THE FANTASTIC PAINTINGS OF
CHARLES
&
WILLIAM
HEATH
ROBINSON

Edited by David Larkin

Introduction by Leo John De Freitas

A Peacock Press/Bantam Book
Toronto * New York * London

We are most grateful to the publishers, libraries, museums and private
collectors who have kindly allowed the use of material in their copyright.

CHARLES & WILLIAM HEATH ROBINSON

PRINTING HISTORY:
First Edition: August, 1976

Published simultaneously in the United States and Canada

PRINTED IN ITALY BY MONDADORI, VERONA

By the 1890s illustrative art in Great Britain had been established long enough so that there was a sound tradition upon which to build. The illustrated journals and newspapers which had begun in the early years of the Victorian period had multiplied in number tremendously, and book publishers too had responded to the demands for illustrated literature. It was possible for young illustrators in the last decade of the nineteenth century to have at least one, if not two, generations of illustrators preceding them in their families. The Robinsons were one such family.

Collectively speaking they could be called the Heath Robinsons (although Charles Robinson, one of the subjects of this book, was not christened with his mother's maiden name), and it is under this composite surname that William Heath Robinson's claim to fame may be found in English dictionaries. Although this present selection of color illustrations does not offer an example of the 'Heath Robinson contraption' that made him famous, suggestions of his later whimsical work are to be found.

Charles Robinson (1870-1937) and William Heath Robinson (1872-1944) were the second and third sons in a large family of four boys and two girls, and they lived for the greater part of their lives in London. Their father had been an illustrator on the *Penny Illustrated Paper*, and their uncle a well-respected artist on the *Illustrated London News* as well as being an illustrator of one or two books. Their grandfather had been a wood engraver on *The London Journal* and *Good Words*, where.he engraved the work of some of the best artists of the day. Therefore, it is easy to appreciate why the brothers should want to turn their natural artistic skills in the direction of illustrative art; as a family tradition it was in their blood. Will attended the Royal Academy schools as a student, while Charles, who had to work as an apprentice in a printing establishment during the day, could attend only evening classes. Yet,

as their work shows, Will's intrinsic skills were not affected by academicism, nor did Charles suffer from his lack of a formal art training.

It is with some regret that the work of their elder brother, Thomas Heath Robinson (1869-1950), could not be included in this collection. The three brothers delighted in being known as the 'Three Musketeers,' and much of their early adult life was spent together in their father's studio, and later in studios shared with one another. Tom, more than either of his brothers, was a 'black-and-white' artist, working in pen and ink for most of his long life, and the relatively small quantity of colored illustrations he executed were, unhappily, not always sympathetically handled by publishers and printers. Although he illustrated many books, the majority of his

drawings are to be found in illustrated journals for boys where the excitement and action of adventure stories were given enthusiastic graphic form by his facile pen.

Of the two brothers Charles and Will, it was Charles who achieved acclaim and popularity first. While still a young man, his black-and-white illustrations to Robert Louis Stevenson's *A Child's Garden of Verses* (1895) were favorably received on both sides of the Atlantic. From then on he became associated, in the public's mind, with a quaint and sympathetic depiction of childhood – especially the infant years. His illustrations to nursery rhymes, fables and fairy stories are invariably gentle and reassuring. Not only was his attitude toward illustrating for young children a carefully considered one, his

painting and drawing techniques were in themselves controlled and refined in such a manner as to admit of nothing harsh. Take, for example, two potentially frightening subjects – one from Thumberline and the other from Hansel and Grethel.

In *The little fishes and Thumberline* (plate 3) we have tiny Thumberline marooned on a lily-pad waiting helplessly while the ugly frog she is being forced to marry is away. The fish (who are soon to nibble through the stem of the plant and so float our heroine off to freedom) bob up and down looking at the diminutive beauty, and even if we have forgotten the story we can suspect, by the delicacy with which Charles has treated the event, that all is soon to be favorably resolved. At this point compare Will's two illustrations to the same story (although in this edition of Hans Andersen's fairy stories the story is entitled 'Tommelise') : *She stood at the door and begged for a piece of barley-corn* (plate 16) and '*Yes, I will go with thee!' said Tommelise, and she seated herself on the bird's back* (plate 17). The comparison will show firstly that both brothers created individual heroines (the Thumberline of Charles is rather more delicate than Will's), and secondly that both artists had the ability to draw convincing natural-history subjects (the field-mice, swallows and fish) in imaginative fairy story settings.

Again in Charles' *Hansel and Grethel in the forest* (plate 4) a possibly sinister or frightening event is 'beautified' and removed from the nightmarish scene it might have been. Lost in the depths of the forest, their plans for escape unintentionally destroyed by the birds, who

have eaten their escape-trail of bread crumbs, the two children stand in the evening shadows of the massive trees. Certainly there is an air of apprehensiveness about the illustration, but everything is too refined and balanced for there to be any real threat to the unfortunate children.

Will too felt a responsibility toward the children for whom he drew.
Commenting on his work for children's books, he compared its humor to the more tongue-in-cheek humor of his work intended for adults:

In my work for children, this [adult] humor is sometimes, although not often, expressed, but the cynicism, I hope, is entirely absent. The opportunities it gives for decorative design and color are infinite.

When using the word 'cynicism' I do so only in a perfectly good-humored sense, but I feel that even in this sense it should not be introduced to children. It is a somewhat oblique way of looking at things and as such is the very reverse of what we should encourage in children.

It might all sound rather paternalistic and even dogmatic. Fatherly, rather than paternalistic, perhaps (both brothers were devoted family men with large families), but dogmatic never. The Robinsons were incapable of extremism in any guise.

But who knows the right way to appeal to children? I confess I have yet to convince myself as to this.

So concluded Will in these comments upon his own approach to illustrating for children.

Sometime before the outbreak of world war in 1914 Will began to draw the incredible devices that were to make his name a household word. (Will's equivalent in the United States was Ruben 'Rube' Lucius Goldberg whose own creation, the ingenious inventor Professor Lucifer Butts, would have had the greatest admiration for Will's contraptions.) The war itself gave an impetus to Will's graphic inventions, with soldiers in the trenches writing to congratulate him on his highly amusing ideas for winning the war, and to suggest further zany machines he might like to design for the war effort (e.g. a 'Practical Mine Finder' and the famous 'Barb Mortar'). As public taste

would have it, Will has generally been remembered for this humorous, inventive work, while his colorful and decorative illustrations have hitherto found only a second place in any collection of his work. Here, in this collection, they take pride of place.

One might wonder whether he resented having to devote so much of his art to this facetious work, and whether he thought it a sacrifice. Certainly he found it hard work leading a sort of dual life as an illustrator, but it would appear that he did not entirely object. He is quoted as saying:

Yet I cannot altogether complain. My humorous work has been a very satisfactory means of expressing what I hope is an original humorous outlook on life.

That this original humor found expression in some of his illustrations for children can be seen in the example taken from *Bill the Minder* (1912), a book which he both wrote and illustrated. In *The King of Troy was compelled to ask his way* (plate 9) the meeting between the sensible and obviously well-mannered children and the flamboyant, crazy-looking old monarch, loaded down with such an odd assortment of things, seems not at all impossible. Will was brilliant at creating the scene in which the unlikely and improbable become quite acceptable and indeed quite logical! Here there is an almost complete reversal of characters. The children are quite composed in manner and sober in dress, while the king (who has been deposed for being frivolous and fun-loving) is anything but regal and aloof. In his later 'contraptions' Will would make use of bits of knotted string, bent nails and oddments of materials ingeniously combined, and surely the massive patchwork bundle on the king's back, tied up with yards and yards of rope and adorned with kettle, pot and umbrella, is suggestive of the artist's future work. It is more than this, of course, as it comments on the artist's fertile mind and the amusement he obviously found in combining the most unlikely of things in his illustrations. Again, the sand-timer and scissors dangling like pendants from the king's neck and the heavy crown tied onto his head are all very characteristic of Will's humor.

Both brothers were to illustrate works other than those for children – for example, poetry. Charles' illustrations to *The Songs and Sonnets of William Shakespeare* (1915) and Will's illustrations to Kipling's *A Song of the English* (1909) show how well they understood the particular problems of perhaps one should say decorating, rather than illustrating, the works of poets. Neither of the illustrators has tried to improve upon the poets' imagery, but instead they have taken the opportunity to express their own feelings toward the poems rather than try to give graphic form to the feelings of the poets. *In the court of love* (plate 36) by Charles, a decorative piece of fancy, delights in the exotic with a gentle sensuousness. Whether the sonnet has been illustrated in any literal fashion or not ('Mine eye and heart are at mental war/ How to decide the conquest of thy sight') does not seem to matter. The painting pleases the eye as the words please the ear. From the same volume Charles depicts a young and enigmatic personification of Time, *I will be true, despite thy scythe and thee* (plate 38), passing before the reader with his arms full of the symbols of Time. Again we can enjoy the artist's work knowing he has not attempted the profane, and admire the design for its balance and decorative appeal.

Will's illustrations to Kipling's work are somewhat more literal interpretations, but then the poems in *A Song of the English* admit of this. I consider *The wrecks dissolve above us| Their dust drops down from afar—| Down to the dark, to the utter dark,| Where the blind white sea snakes are* (plate 2) a wonderfully imaginative illustration to the poem with the unpromising title of 'The deep-sea cables.' There is a silence, and a melancholy, as well as a sense of inevitability about the old sailing boat slowly disintegrating in the element which had once offered her a livelihood. The mast and spars slowly sink into the stillness expressed in the following line of the poem:

> There is no sound, no echo of sound,
> in the deserts of the deep.

For an interesting contrast compare the stillness of decay expressed in this illustration with the excitement and vitality with which the artist has drawn the *Revenge* engaged in battle in *When Drake went down to the Horn and England was crowned thereby* (plate 1).

The illustrations reproduced here are practically all taken from first editions of gift books, publications which thrived in the early years of this century before 1914. The gift book was a successful venture at the time by publishers who wanted to provide something extra-special for Christmas. They were large, lavishly illustrated tomes, and generally dressed in rich red bindings with ornate gold-blocked designs across the front cover and spine. The special feature of these works was the selection of colored plates to be found in the text, and I imagine that part of the success and later decline of this type of book can be explained by the book-buying public's initial thrill with and subsequent indifference to well-reproduced color plates.

Although primarily 'special Christmas fare,' gift books were of course the ideal present to give on any special occasion and consequently the best popular artists were employed in their illustration and decoration. Edmund Dulac and Arthur Rackham were well represented, and so, of course, were Charles Robinson and William Heath Robinson. In part the illustrations before you show how the Robinson brothers responded, in their own ways, to the idea behind the gift book, and how well they succeeded in carrying their light-hearted and beautiful interpretations of fantasy worlds into people's homes.

Leo John De Freitas
August 1975

1) W. Heath Robinson
When Drake went down to the Horn
and England was crowned thereby.

Song of the English

HODDER & STOUGHTON

1909

W HEATH ROBINSON

2) W. Heath Robinson

The wrecks dissolve above us,
their dust drops down from afar –
Down to the dark, to the utter dark,
where the blind white sea-snakes are.

Song of the English

HODDER & STOUGHTON

1909

3) Charles Robinson, R.I.

The little fishes and Thumberline.

The Big Book of Fairy Tales

BLACKIE & SON

1911

4) Charles Robinson, R.I.

Hansel and Grethel in the forest.

The Big Book of Fairy Tales

BLACKIE & SON

1911

5) Charles Robinson, R.I.

The frog fetches the golden ball.

The Big Book of Fairy Tales

BLACKIE & SON

1911

6) Frontispiece

Bill the Minder

Written and Illustrated by
W. Heath Robinson

CONSTABLE & CO.

1912

7) And left him to have his cry out.

Bill the Minder

Written and Illustrated by
W. Heath Robinson

CONSTABLE & CO.

1912

8) They came upon a great stone sphinx.

Bill the Minder

Written and Illustrated by
W. Heath Robinson

CONSTABLE & CO.

1912

9) The King of Troy compelled to ask his way.

Bill the Minder

Written and Illustrated by
W. Heath Robinson

CONSTABLE & CO.

1912

10) Charles Robinson, R.I.

Spring

THE ILLUSTRATED LONDON NEWS

Christmas 1912

CHARLES ROBINSON

11) Charles Robinson, R.I.

Summer

THE ILLUSTRATED LONDON NEWS

Christmas 1912

CHARLES ROBINSON

12) Charles Robinson, R.I.

Autumn

THE ILLUSTRATED LONDON NEWS

Christmas 1912

13) Charles Robinson, R.I.

Winter

THE ILLUSTRATED LONDON NEWS

Christmas 1912

14) Charles Robinson, R.I.

He was mourning now, and nothing but purple
flowers must henceforth grow in the garden.

The Four Gardens

WM. HEINEMANN LTD.

1912

15) W. Heath Robinson

The bud opened into full-blown flower,
in the middle of which lay a beautiful child.

The Marsh King's Daughter

Hans Andersen's Fairy Tales

CONSTABLE & CO.

1913

16) W. Heath Robinson

She stood at the door and begged
for a piece of barley-corn.

Tommelise

Hans Andersen's Fairy Tales

CONSTABLE & CO.

1913

17) W. Heath Robinson

"Yes, I will go with thee!" said Tommelise,
and she seated herself on the bird's back.

Tommelise

Hans Andersen's Fairy Tales

CONSTABLE & CO.

1913

18) W. Heath Robinson

Round and round they went,
such whirling and twirling.

Elfin-Mount

Hans Andersen's Fairy Tales

CONSTABLE & CO.

1913

19) W. Heath Robinson

She put the statue in her garden.

The Little Mermaid

Hans Andersen's Fairy Tales

CONSTABLE & CO.

1913

20) W. Heath Robinson

The peasant's wife sat on Sundays at the door
of her cottage reading her hymn-book.

The Wild Swan

Hans Andersen's Fairy Tales

CONSTABLE & CO.

1913

21) W. Heath Robinson

Princesses he found in plenty, but whether
they were real princesses it was impossible
for him to decide.

The Real Princess

Hans Andersen's Fairy Tales

CONSTABLE & CO.

1913

22) W. Heath Robinson

The swineherd scolded and the rain poured down.

The Swineherd

Hans Andersen's Fairy Tales

CONSTABLE & CO.

1913

23) W. Heath Robinson

He jumped down from the old man's lap
and danced around him on the floor.

The Naughty Boy

Hans Andersen's Fairy Tales

CONSTABLE & CO.

1913

24) Charles Robinson, R.I.

He folded his arms and leaned forward till
his eyes looked into John's.

Margaret's Book
by H. Fielding-Hall

HUTCHINSON & CO.

1913

25) Charles Robinson, R.I.

"I don't think your name can be Margaret,"
said Perch, "you don't look like Margaret."

Margaret's Book
by H. Fielding-Hall

HUTCHINSON & CO.

1913

26) Charles Robinson, R.I.

He said, "I am surprised, I expect it's
a party; it's lucky I woke."

Margaret's Book
by H. Fielding-Hall

HUTCHINSON & CO.

1913

27) Charles Robinson, R.I.

There was a lovely fairy in the air,
just in front of . . .

Margaret's Book
by H. Fielding-Hall

HUTCHINSON & CO.

1913

28) Charles Robinson, R.I.

She felt herself changing.

Margaret's Book
by H. Fielding-Hall

HUTCHINSON & CO.

1913

30) Charles Robinson, R.I.

The King of the Mountains of the Moon.

Frontispiece

The Happy Prince and
Other Tales by Oscar Wilde

DUCKWORTH & CO.

1913

31) Charles Robinson, R.I.

"Let the fireworks begin," said the King.

The Remarkable Rocket

The Happy Prince and
Other Tales by Oscar Wilde

DUCKWORTH & CO.

1913

32) W. Heath Robinson

Overon. "And make him with fair ægle break his faith."

A Midsummer Night's Dream

CONSTABLE & CO.

1914

33) W. Heath Robinson

Hippolyta. "Four days will quickly steep
themselves in night."

A Midsummer Night's Dream

CONSTABLE & CO.

1914

34) W. Heath Robinson

Fairy. "She never had so sweet a changeling."

A Midsummer Night's Dream

CONSTABLE & CO.

1914

35) W. Heath Robinson

Bottom. "Why do they turn away?
This is knavery of them to make me afeared."

A Midsummer Night's Dream

CONSTABLE & CO.

1914

36) Charles Robinson, R.I.

In the court of love.

The Songs and Sonnets
of William Shakespeare

DUCKWORTH & CO.

1915

37) Charles Robinson, R.I.

On a day – alack the day! –
Love, whose month is ever May,
Spied a blossom passing fair
Playing in the wanton air;

The Songs and Sonnets
of William Shakespeare

DUCKWORTH & CO.

1915

CHARLES ROBINSON

38) Charles Robinson, R.I.

I will be true,
despite thy scythe and thee.

The Songs and Sonnets
of William Shakespeare

DUCKWORTH & CO.

1915

39) W. Heath Robinson

Every evening the beast paid her a visit.

Old Time Stories
by Charles Perrault

CONSTABLE & CO.

1921

40) W. Heath Robinson

The most beautiful sight he had ever seen.

Old Time Stories
by Charles Perrault

CONSTABLE & CO.

1921